D1456831

George
Herbert

HERBERT'S WORKS

A one-volume Works of George Herbert, *ed. F.E. Hutchinson, is published by Clarendon, 1941 (corrected 1978). This includes:*

The Temple: *Sacred Poems and Private Ejaculations*
English Poems *in the Williams MS not included in The Temple*

Poems *from Walton's* Lives

Doubtful Poems

A priest to the Temple, The Country Parson

Various Translations

Outlandish Proverbs

Jacula Prudentum

Letters
plus various writings in Latin

See also The English Poems of George Herbert *ed. C.A. Patrides, Dent, 1974*

For Herbert's life, see Izaac Walton, Four Lives *and John Aubrey,* Brief Lives.

There are a number of helpful introductions to Herbert and his work, among them:

T.S. Eliot, George Herbert *(Writers and their Work, No. 152, 1962).*

D.J. Enright, 'George Herbert and the Devotional Poets', From Donne to Marvell, *ed. Boris Ford, 1956.*

Helen Gardner, Introduction to World Classics edition of George Herbert, 1961.

Rosemond Tuve, A Reading of George Herbert, *Chicago, 1952.*

POETS AND PROPHETS

A selection of poems by

George Herbert

THE LENTEN POET

exploring his pilgrimage

of faith

CHOSEN AND

INTRODUCED BY

RUTH ETCHELLS

A LION BOOK

Tring • Batavia • Sydney

Published by
Lion Publishing plc
Icknield Way, Tring, Herts, England
ISBN 0 7459 1386 5
Lion Publishing Corporation
1705 Hubbard Avenue, Batavia, Illinois 60510, USA
ISBN 0 7459 1386 5
Albatross Books Pty Ltd
PO Box 320, Sutherland, NSW 2232, Australia
ISBN 0 86760 925 7

First edition 1988

Herbert's poems are taken from *The Temple*, ed. C.A. Patrides, Everyman, 1974

British Library Cataloguing in Publication Data

Herbert, George, *1593-1633*
    Selections from the poetry of George Herbert,
    the Lenten poet, exploring his
    pilgrimage of faith.—(Poets and
    prophets).
    I. Title   II. Etchells, Ruth   III. Series
    821'.3
ISBN 0-7459-1386-5

Library of Congress Cataloging in Publication Data

Herbert, George, 1593–1633 (Poets and prophets)
    Bibliography: p.
    ISBN 0-7459-1386-5
    1. Lent—Poetry.   2. Christian poetry, English.   I. Etchells,
    Ruth.   II. Title.
    PR3507 A4 1988
    821'.3—dc19

Printed in Italy

CONTENTS

INTRODUCTION

George Herbert was born in 1593, in Montgomery in Wales, in the same year as his most famous biographer, Izaac Walton. One of a family of ten children, his background was both cultured and courtly, and he was fortunate enough to be born at a time when the English language and its literature was reaching perhaps its finest flowering. He was ten years old when Queen Elizabeth I died, and in those ten years Sidney and Spenser were both publishing some of their most important work, John Donne was beginning to write his powerful and witty love poetry, and Shakespeare was producing *The Merchant of Venice, Julius Caesar, Henry V* and *Twelfth Night*. These were forging the language of Herbert the poet. Just as significantly for George Herbert, who was to become a clergyman of the Church of England (what he called 'The British Church'), Lancelot Andrewes—a spiritual giant with a mastery of language—had been appointed Dean of Westminster.

In 1612, when Herbert was nineteen and first publishing verse (two Latin Poems in memory of the death of James I's heir apparent, Prince Henry), Oliver Cromwell was just thirteen and John Milton a four-year-old child. Herbert's later poetry reflects the deep divisions in church and nation in which these two played so dramatic a part. But Herbert's verse was probably much more deeply shaped by another influence, The King James ('Authorized') Version of the Bible, published in 1611.

These three things—the high literary culture of his age, the life of the Church of England, and national affairs focussed in the Royal Court and the patronage of the King—shaped the context in which the poet made those decisions which form the material for his most moving poetry.

Herbert was highly gifted. By the time he was twenty-three he was elected to a major Fellowship of Trinity College, Cambridge, At twenty-five he was appointed Reader in Rhetoric in Cambridge and two years later he was elected Public Orator there, a distinction he held for eight years. In 1624—halfway through his Public Oratorship—he was also elected MP for Montgomery. There seemed no doubt that he had attracted attention in the highest places: a distinguished public career lay before him.

What followed we can only guess from some of his poems and from the account of Nicolas Ferrars, one of his closest friends and the leader of the Christian community settled at Little Gidding. Ferrars wrote the preface to Herbert's poems when they were first published in 1633, after Herbert's death. He speaks of Herbert 'quitting both his deserts and all opportunities... choosing rather to serve at God's Altar, than to seek the honour of State-employments'. And he makes it clear that this was a decision Herbert made in response, not to any external pressure, but to 'inward inforcements', that is, an inner compulsion so strong that he resolutely left behind him the glittering public life which was his for the taking. Instead, in 1626 he was ordained in the Church of England, associating himself with the life of Little Gidding from his first 'living', four miles away. Four years later, a year after his marriage, he became Rector of the little parish of Bemerton, near Salisbury. He had been there only three years when he died, just before his fortieth birthday.

Herbert's poems record the struggle which lay behind this course of action—and the peace and spiritual richness which followed. Ferrars records Herbert's sense of calling to God's service: 'His faithful discharge was such as may make him justly a companion to the primitive saints, and a pattern or more for the age he lived in.' Such a close walk with God is always costly, and Herbert's poem 'Deniall' speaks honestly of his anguish:

> O that Thou should'st give dust a tongue
>   To crie to Thee,
> And then not heare it crying! all day long
>   My heart was in my knee,
>   But no hearing.

But he won through, and this present selection of poems is a record of that victory. His own account of his poems is that they record 'many spiritual conflicts betwixt God and my Soul, before I could subject mine to the will of *Jesus my Master*: in Whose service I have now found perfect freedom'.

Rather than put at risk his spiritual life, Herbert turned aside from the corridors of power which might have been his. But he took with him to the humble position he had chosen, all his brilliant gifts. And he uses his poetic skill, his marvellous turn of phrase, his ability to create verbal music, his vivid sense of image, and his daring verbal wit, to create the melodious and moving miniatures for which he is best known.

He retained his pleasure, too, in highly compressed proverbial wit, as these lines from 'Charms and Knots' make plain:

> ...'Who shuts his hand, hath lost his gold:
> Who opens it, hath it twice told.
>
> Who goes to bed and doth not pray,
> Maketh two nights to ev'ry day.
>
> Who by aspersions throw a stone
> At th' head of others, hit their own'

Herbert's whole course of life was a kind of Lent (the weeks before Easter which Christians use as a time of spiritual discipline and re-appraisal): a discipline joyfully and firmly accepted in order the better to prepare him to serve his Lord, and to enter more fully those courts of God's praise where his heart truly lay. In order to explore this, I have arranged the selection of his poetry in the framework of the Ash Wednesday Collect (the set prayer for the first day of Lent) as he would have known it. His Lent was as glad as it was disciplined, and the tone of his verse ranges from contrition to delight: but his test of obedience in the end was that it should be lived out, not simply reflected on. His testimony was that when any man or woman did so, they were seized with so deep a sense of God's mercies that all sense of loss or self-imposed austerity fell away, and God himself became 'such a Life as killeth *death*', 'such a Heart, as joyes in love'.

The Collect for the First Day of Lent, *according to the Book of Common Prayer, 1559*

Almighty and everlasting God, which hatest nothing that Thou hast made, and dost forgive the sins of all them that be penitent: Create and make in us new and contrite hearts, that we worthily lamenting our sins, and knowledging our wretchedness, may obtain of Thee, the God of all mercy, perfect remission and forgiveness: through Jesus Christ.

PROLOGUE

These lines from the poem 'Lent', express the spirit of discipline, of striving for obedience to God, which lies behind the whole shape of Herbert's poetry. This 'Lenten spirit' combines sober realism about the limits of human effort with the poet's trustfulness in the God who may 'turn and take me by the hand'; and who will certainly, as we shall see in this selection of verse, lead the poet through the Lenten disciplines of his life to peace of spirit and ease of soul.

It's true, we cannot reach Christs forti'th day;
Yet to go part of that religious way
      Is better then to rest:
We cannot reach our Saviours puritie;
Yet are we bid, *Be holy ev'n as he.*
      In both let's do our best.

Who goeth in the way which Christ hath gone,
Is much more sure to meet with him, then one
      That travelleth by-wayes:
Perhaps my God, though he be farre before,
May turn, and take me by the hand, and more
      May strengthen my decayes.

Yet Lord instruct us to improve our fast
By starving sinne and taking such repast,
      As may our faults controll:
That ev'ry man may revell at his doore,
Not in his parlour; banquetting the poore,
      And among those his soul.

GOD OF MERCY, GOD OF LOVE

All Herbert's poems, whether questioning God, struggling with him, or rejoicing in him, assume certain things. One is the conviction that the God who is beyond time and all-powerful is a forgiving and caring Creator. He actively seeks to set right anyone or anything in his creation which has chosen a wrong way. For Herbert, God's present relationship with his creatures is one of tenderness as much as of judgement, of re-making rather than of condemning. This is part of the love which Herbert sees as God's very nature. It is the mainspring of creation and beyond it of the world of heaven and its angels. This is the love which draws from Herbert songs of praise and delight, as well as of penitence and obedience.

F·R·O·M

GIDDINESSE

Lord, mend or rather make us: one creation
    Will not suffice our turn:
Except thou make us dayly, we shall spurn
    Our own salvation.

Cho.   Let all the world in ev'ry corner sing,
        My God and King

Vers.   The heav'ns are not too high,
        His praise may thither flie:
        The earth is not too low,
        His praises there may grow.

Cho.   Let all the world in ev'ry corner sing,
        My God and King

Vers.   The Church with psalms must shout,
        No doore can keep them out:
        But above all, the heart
        Must bear the longest part.

Cho.   Let all the world in ev'ry corner sing,
        My God and King

Chor.	Praised be the God of love,
Men	Here below,
Angels	And here above:
Chor.	Who hath dealt his mercies so,
Angels	To his friend,
Men	And to his foe;
Chor.	That both grace and glorie tend
Angels	Us of old,
Men	And us in th'end
Chor.	The greatest shepherd of the fold
Angels	Us did make,
Men	For us was sold.
Chor.	He our foes in pieces brake;
Angels	Him we touch;
Men	And him we take.
Chor.	Wherefore since that he is such,
Angels	We adore,
Men	And we do crouch.
Chor.	Lord, thy praises should be more.
Angels	We have none,
Men	And we no store.
Chor.	Praised be the God alone,
	Who hath made of two folds one.

A number of writers of this period used intellectually witty or outrageous images and visual effects in the shape of their poems to express deep feeling. In this poem, the shortening shape of the verses is a picture of the work of God as a good Gardener, pruning and shaping men and women, his tender plants, to make them grow strong and true.

I blesse thee, Lord, because I G R O W
Among thy trees, which in a   R O W
To thee both fruit and order   O W.

What open force, or hidden   C H A R M
Can blast my fruit, or bring me H A R M,
While the inclosure is thine   A R M?

Inclose me still for fear I   S T A R T.
Be to me rather sharp and   T A R T,
Than let me want thy hand & A R T.

When thou dost greater judgements   S P A R E
And with thy knife but prune and   P A R E,
Ev'n fruitfull trees more fruitfull   A R E.

Such sharpnes shows the sweetest   F R E N D:
Such cuttings rather heal than   R E N D:
And such beginnings touch their   E N D.

NEW AND CONTRITE HEARTS

In Herbert's poetry it is always God who moves us to good actions. So in these poems he prays that God will so touch and change hearts, that their hardness will soften and repentance (a turning away from wrong) and a clear sense of the need for penitence will follow.

VANITIE II

Poore silly soul, whose hope and head lies low;
Whose flat delights on earth do creep and grow;
To whom the starres shine not so fair, as eyes;
Nor solid work, as false embroyderies;
Hark and beware, lest what you now do measure
And write for sweet, prove a most sowre displeasure.

O heare betimes, lest thy relenting
   May come too late!
To purchase heaven for repenting,
   Is no hard rate.
If souls be made of earthly mold,
   Let them love gold;
   If born on high,
Let them unto their kindred flie:
For they can never be at rest,
   Till they regain their ancient nest.
Then silly soul take heed; for earthly joy
Is but a bubble, and makes thee a boy.

Full of rebellion, I would die,
Or fight, or travell, or denie
That thou hast ought to do with me.
O tame my heart;
It is thy highest art
To captivate strong holds to thee.

If thou shalt let this venome lurk,
And in suggestions fume and work,
My soul will turn to bubbles straight,
And thence by kinde
Vanish into a winde,
Making thy workmanship deceit.

O smooth my rugged heart, and there
Engrave thy rev'rend law and fear;
Or make a new one, since the old
Is saplesse grown,
And a much fitter stone
To hide my dust, then thee to hold.

The circumstances of Herbert's life were not distressing in any dramatic sense and yet so much of his poetry is about affliction—this is because it records the struggles of his inner life as he grows in saintliness and wrestles with God in order to do so.

When first thou didst entice to thee my heart,
        I thought the service brave:
So many joyes I writ down for my part,
        Besides what I might have
Out of my stock of naturall delights,
Augmented with thy gracious benefits.

I looked on thy furniture so fine,
        And made it fine to me:
Thy glorious houshold-stuffe did me entwine,
        And 'tice me unto thee.
Such starres I counted mine: both heav'n and earth
Payd me my wages in a world of mirth.

What pleasures could I want, whose King I served?
        Where joyes my fellows were.
Thus argu'd into hopes, my thoughts reserved
        No place for grief or fear.
Therefore my sudden soul caught at the place,
And made her youth and fiercenesse seek thy face.

At first thou gav'st me milk and sweetnesses;
        I had my wish and way:
My dayes were straw'd with flow'rs and happinesse;
        There was no moneth but May.
But with my yeares sorrow did twist and grow,
And made a partie unawares for wo.

My flesh began unto my soul in pain,
        Sicknesses cleave my bones;
Consuming agues dwell in ev'ry vein,
        And tune my breath to grones.
Sorrow was all my soul; I scarce beleeved,
Till grief did tell me roundly, that I lived.

When I got health, thou took'st away my life,
   And more; for my friends die:
My mirth and edge was lost; a blunted knife
   Was of more use then I.
Thus thinne and lean without a fence or friend,
I was blown through with ev'ry storm and winde.

Whereas my birth and spirit rather took
   The way that takes the town;
Thou didst betray me to a lingring book,
   And wrap me in a gown.
I was entangled in the world of strife,
Before I had the power to change my life.

Yet, for I threatned oft the siege to raise,
   Not simpring all mine age,
Thou often didst with Academick praise
   Melt and dissolve my rage.
I took thy sweetned pill, till I came where
I could not go away, nor persevere.

Yet lest perchance I should too happie be
   In my unhappinesse,
Turning my purge to food, thou throwest me
   Into more sicknesses.
Thus doth thy power crosse-bias me, not making
Thine own gift good, yet me from my wayes taking.

Now I am here, what thou wilt do with me
   None of my books will show:
I reade, and sigh, and wish I were a tree;
   For sure then I should grow
To fruit or shade: at least some bird would trust
Her houshold to me, and I should be just.

Yet, though thou troublest me, I must be meek;
   In weaknesse must be stout.
Well, I will change the service, and go seek
   Some other master out.
Ah my deare God! though I am clean forgot,
Let me not love thee, if I love thee not.

AFFLICTION III

My heart did heave, and there came forth, *O God!*
By that I knew that thou wast in the grief,
To guide and govern it to my relief,
    Making a scepter of the rod:
      Hadst thou not had thy part,
Sure the unruly sigh had broke my heart.

But since thy breath gave me both life and shape,
Thou knowst my tallies; and when there's assign'd
So much breath to a sigh, what's then behinde?
    O if some yeares with it escape,
      The sigh then onely is
A gale to bring me sooner to my blisse.

Thy life on earth was grief, and thou art still
Constant unto it, making it to be
A point of honour, now to grieve in me,
    And in thy members suffer ill.
      They who lament one crosse,
Thou dying dayly, praise thee to thy losse.

I struck the board, and cry'd, No more.
                I will abroad.
        What? shall I ever sigh and pine?
My lines and life are free; free as the rode,
        Loose as the winde, as large as store.
                Shall I be still in suit?
        Have I no harvest but a thorn
        To let me bloud, and not restore
What I have lost with cordiall fruit?
                Sure there was wine
    Before my sighs did drie it: there was corn
        Before my tears did drown it.
        Is the yeare onely lost to me?
        Have I no bayes to crown it?
No flowers, no garlands gay? all blasted?
                All wasted?
        Not so, my heart: but there is fruit,
                And thou hast hands.
        Recover all thy sigh-blown age
On double pleasures: leave thy cold dispute
Of what is fit, and not forsake thy cage,
                Thy rope of sands,
Which pettie thoughts have made, and made to thee
        Good cable, to enforce and draw,
                And be thy law,
        While thou didst wink and wouldst not see.
                Away; take heed:
                I will abroad.
Call in thy deaths head there: tie up thy fears.
                He that forbears
        To suit and serve his need,
                Deserves his load.
But as I rav'd and grew more fierce and wilde
                At every word,
Me thoughts I heard one calling, *Child:*
        And I reply'd, *My Lord.*

CONFESSION

H erbert suggests that, though God can soften the resistance of our hard hearts, there must be an active response on our part. We must be distressed for all that is wrong within us and long for it to be put right. Herbert personalizes this from his own life in the poems that follow.

SINNES ROUND

Sorrie I am, my God, sorrie I am,
That my offences course it in a ring.
My thoughts are working like a busie flame,
Untill their cockatrice they hatch and bring:
And when they once have perfected their draughts,
My words take fire from my inflamed thoughts.

My words take fire from my inflamed thoughts,
Which spit it forth like the Sicilian hill.
They vent the wares, and passe them with their faults,
And by their breathing ventilate the ill.
But words suffice not, where are lewd intentions:
My hands do joyn to finish the inventions.

My hands do joyn to finish the inventions:
And so my sinnes ascend three stories high,
As Babel grew, before there were dissentions.
Yet ill deeds loyter not: for they supplie
New thoughts of sinning: wherefore, to my shame,
Sorrie I am, my God, sorrie I am.

O do not use me
After my sinnes! look not on my desert,
But on thy glorie! then thou wilt reform
And not refuse me: for thou onely art
The mightie God, but I a sillie worm;
             O do not bruise me!

O do not urge me!
For what account can thy ill steward make?
I have abus'd thy stock, destroy'd thy woods,
Suckt all thy magazens: my head did ake,
Till it found out how to consume thy goods:
             O do not scourge me!

O do not blinde me!
I have deserv'd that an Egyptian night
Should thicken all my powers; because my lust
Hath still sow'd fig-leaves to exclude thy light:
But I am frailtie, and already dust;
             O do not grinde me!

O do not fill me
With the turn'd viall of thy bitter wrath!
For thou hast other vessels full of bloud,
A part whereof my Saviour empti'd hath,
Ev'n unto death: since he di'd for my good,
             O do not kill me!

But O reprieve me!
For thou hast *life* and *death* at thy command;
Thou art both *Judge* and *Saviour, Feast* and *rod,*
Cordiall and *Corrosive*: put not thy hand
Into the bitter box; but O my God,
             My God, relieve me!

Broken in pieces all asunder,
>>> Lord, hunt me not,
>>> A thing forgot,
Once a poore creature, now a wonder,
>>> A wonder tortur'd in the space
>>> Betwixt this world and that of grace.

My thoughts are all a case of knives,
>>> Wounding my heart
>>> With scatter'd smart,
As watring pots give flowers their lives.
>>> Nothing their furie can controll,
>>> While they do wound and prick my soul.

All my attendants are at strife,
>>> Quitting their place
>>> Unto my face:
Nothing performs the task of life:
>>> The elements are let loose to fight,
>>> And while I live, trie out their right.

Oh help, my God! let not their plot
>>> Kill them and me,
>>> And also thee,
Who art my life: dissolve the knots
>>> As the sunne scatters by his light
>>> All the rebellions of the night.

Then shall those powers, which work for grief,
>>> Enter thy pay,
>>> And day by day
Labour thy praise, and my relief;
>>> With care and courage building me,
>>> Till I reach heav'n and much more thee.

Lord, I confesse my sinne is great;
Great is my sinne. Oh! gently treat
With thy quick flow'r thy momentarie bloom;
Whose life is still pressing
In one undressing,
A steadie aiming at a tombe.

Mans age is two houres work, or three:
Each day doth round about us see.
Thus are we to delights: but we are all
To sorrows old,
If life be told
From what life feeleth, Adams fall.

O let thy height of mercie then
Compassionate short-breathed men.
Cut me not off for my most foul transgression:
I do confesse
My foolishnesse;
My God, accept of my confession.

Sweeten at length this bitter bowl,
Which thou hast pour'd into my soul;
Thy wormwood turn to health, windes to fair weather:
For if thou stay,
I and this day,
As we did rise, we die together.

When thou for sinne rebukest man,
Forthwith he waxeth wo and wan:
Bitternesse fills our bowels; all our hearts
Pine, and decay,
And drop away,
And carrie with them th' other parts.

But thou wilt sinne and grief destroy;
That so the broken bones may joy,
And tune together in a well-set song,
Full of his praises,
Who dead men raises.
Fractures well cur'd make us more strong.

BITTER-SWEET

Ah my deare angrie Lord,
Since thou dost love, yet strike;
Cast down, yet help afford;
Sure I will do the like.

I will complain, yet praise;
I will bewail, approve:
And all my sowre-sweet dayes
I will lament, and love.

Throw away thy rod,
Throw away thy wrath:
        O my God,
Take the gentle path.

For my hearts desire
Unto thine is bent:
        I aspire
To a full consent.

Not a word or look
I affect to own,
        But by book,
And thy book alone.

Though I fail, I weep:
Though I halt in pace,
        Yet I creep
To the throne of grace.

Then let wrath remove;
Love will do the deed:
        For with love
Stonie hearts will bleed.

Love is swift of foot;
Love's a man of warre,
        And can shoot,
And can hit from farre.

Who can scape his bow?
That which wrought on thee,
        Brought thee low,
Needs must work on me.

Throw away thy rod;
Though man frailties hath,
        Thou art God:
Throw away thy wrath.

FORGIVENESS

The final purpose of Herbert's verse is joy; joy in all that God gives to his creation, joy in the acts of God in human history, joy most of all in the perfect forgiveness and peace that God gives to the struggling heart, through his act of saving love in his Son, Jesus Christ.

LOVE III

Love bade me welcome: yet my soul drew back,
> Guiltie of dust and sinne.
But quick-ey'd Love, observing me grow slack
> From my first entrance in,
Drew nearer to me, sweetly questioning,
> If I lack'd any thing.

A guest, I answer'd, worthy to be here:
> Love said, You shall be he.
I the unkinde, ungratefull? Ah my deare,
> I cannot look on thee.
Love took my hand, and smiling did reply,
> Who made the eyes but I?

Truth Lord, but I have marr'd them: let my shame
> Go where it doth deserve.
And know you not, sayes Love, who bore the blame?
> My deare, then I will serve.
You must sit down, sayes Love, and taste my meat:
> So I did sit and eat.

THE FLOWER

How fresh, O Lord, how sweet and clean
Are thy returns! ev'n as the flowers in spring;
    To which, besides their own demean,
The late-past frosts tributes of pleasure bring.
            Grief melts away
            Like snow in May,
        As if there were no such cold thing.

Who would have thought my shrivel'd heart
Could have recover'd greennesse? It was gone
    Quite under ground; as flowers depart
To see their mother-root, when they have blown;
            Where they together
            All the hard weather,
        Dead to the world, keep house unknown.

These are thy wonders, Lord of power,
Killing and quickning, bringing down to hell
    And up to heaven in an houre;
Making a chiming of a passing-bell.
            We say amisse,
            This or that is:
        Thy word is all, if we could spell.

O that I once past changing were,
Fast in thy Paradise, where no flower can wither!
    Many a spring I shoot up fair,
Offring at heav'n, growing and groning thither:
            Nor doth my flower
            Want a spring-showre,
        My sinnes and I joining together:

But while I grow in a straight line,
Still upwards bent, as if heav'n were mine own,
Thy anger comes, and I decline:
What frost to that? what pole is not the zone,
Where all things burn,
When thou dost turn,
And the least frown of thine is shown?

And now in age I bud again,
After so many deaths I live and write;
I once more smell the dew and rain,
And relish versing: O my onely light,
It cannot be
That I am he
On whom thy tempests fell all night.

These are thy wonders, Lord of love,
To make us see we are but flowers that glide:
Which when we once can finde and prove,
Thou hast a garden for us, where to bide.
Who would be more,
Swelling through store,
Forfeit their Paradise by their pride.

This, like many of Herbert's poems, so expresses Christian experience that it has become a well-loved and enduring hymn.

> King of Glorie, King of Peace,
> I will love thee;
> And that love may never cease,
> I will move thee.
>
> Thou has granted my request,
> Thou hast heard me:
> Thou didst note my working breast,
> Thou hast spar'd me.
>
> Wherefore with my utmost art
> I will sing thee,
> And the cream of all my heart
> I will bring thee.
>
> Though my sinnes against me cried,
> Thou didst cleare me;
> And alone, when they replied,
> Thou didst heare me.
>
> Sev'n whole dayes, not one in seven,
> I will praise thee.
> In my heart, though not in heaven,
> I can raise thee.
>
> Thou grew'st soft and moist with tears,
> Thou relentedst:
> And when Justice call'd for fears,
> Thou dissentedst.
>
> Small it is, in this poore sort
> To enroll thee:
> Ev'n eternitie is too short
> To extoll thee.

JESUS

In the more modern version of the Lenten Collect, the last phrase, 'through Jesus Christ', is expanded by the words, 'who is alive and reigns with you and the Holy Spirit, one God now and for ever'. The Jesus of whom Herbert writes is indeed to him both a dying Saviour and a risen Lord, one who gives his life and yet reigns in glory. The simple words 'through Jesus Christ' convey for the poet all this and much more, as the following poems show.

JESU

JESU is in my heart, his sacred name
Is deeply carved there: but th'other week
A great affliction broke the little frame,
Ev'n all to pieces: which I went to seek:
And first I found the corner, where was J,
After, where ES, and next where U was graved.
When I had got these parcels, instantly
I sat me down to spell them, and perceived
That to my broken heart he was *I ease you*,
    and to my whole is JESU

REDEMPTION

Having been tenant long to a rich Lord,
    Not thriving, I resolved to be bold,
    And make a suit unto him, to afford
A new small-rented lease, and cancell th' old.

In heaven at his manour I him sought:
    They told me there, that he was lately gone
    About some land, which he had dearly bought
Long since on earth, to take possession.

I straight return'd, and knowing his great birth,
    Sought him accordingly in great resorts;
    In cities, theatres, gardens, parks, and courts:
At length I heard a ragged noise and mirth

    Of theeves and murderers: there I him espied,
    Who straight, *Your suit is granted,* said, & died.

O my chief good,
How shall I measure out thy bloud?
How shall I count what thee befell,
 And each grief tell?

Shall I thy woes
Number according to thy foes?
Or, since one starre show'd thy first breath,
 Shall all thy death?

Or shall each leaf,
Which falls in Autumne, score a grief?
Or cannot leaves, but fruit, be signe
 Of the true vine?

Then let each houre
Of my whole life one grief devoure;
That thy distresse through all may runne,
 And be my sunne.

Or rather let
My severall sinnes their sorrows get;
That as each beast his cure doth know,
 Each sinne may so.

Since bloud is fittest, Lord, to write
Thy sorrows in, and bloudie fight;
My heart hath store, write there, where in
One box doth lie both ink and sinne;

That when sinne spies so many foes,
Thy whips, thy nails, thy wounds, thy woes,
All come to lodge there, sinne may say,
No room for me, and flie away.

Sinne being gone, oh fill the place,
And keep possession with thy grace;
Lest sinne take courage and return,
And all the writings blot or burn.

THE DAWNING

Awake sad heart, whom sorrow ever drowns;
    Take up thine eyes, which feed on earth;
Unfold thy forehead gather'd into frowns:
    Thy Saviour comes, and with him mirth:
        Awake, awake;
And with a thankfull heart his comforts take.
    But thou dost still lament, and pine, and crie;
    And feel his death, but not his victorie.

Arise sad heart; if thou dost not withstand,
    Christs resurrection thine may be:
Do not by hanging down break from the hand,
    Which as it riseth, raiseth thee:
        Arise, arise;
And with his buriall-linen drie thine eyes:
    Christ left his grave-clothes, that we might, when
      grief
    Draws tears, or bloud, not want an handkerchief.

_____ Easter Wings _____

Lord, who createdst man in wealth and store,
Though foolishly he lost the same,
Decaying more and more,
Till he became
Most poore:
With thee
O let me rise
As larks, harmoniously,
And sing this day thy victories:
Then shall the fall further the flight in me.

My tender age in sorrow did beginne:
And still with sicknesses and shame
Thou didst so punish sinne,
That I became
Most thinne.
With thee
Let me combine,
And feel this day thy victorie:
For, if I imp my wing on thine,
Affliction shall advance the flight in me.

THE JOY OF OBEDIENCE

The poems in this section focus on the life of obedience to God—at the personal level, through prayer and feeding on the Scriptures; and through the church's worship, day by day and in the great Christian festivals.

F·R·O·M
AN OFFERING

...Since my sadnesse
Into gladnesse
Lord thou dost convert,
O accept
What thou hast kept,
As thy due desert.

Had I many,
Had I any,
(For this heart is none)
All were thine
And none of mine:
Surely thine along.

Yet thy favour
May give savour
To this poore oblation;
And it raise
To be thy praise,
And be my salvation.

Teach me, my God and King,
In all things thee to see,
And what I do in any thing,
To do it as for thee:

Not rudely, as a beast,
To runne into an action;
But still to make thee prepossest,
And give it his perfection.

A man that looks on glasse,
On it may stay his eye;
Or if he pleaseth, through it passe,
And then the heav'n espie.

All may of thee partake:
Nothing can be so mean,
Which with this tincture (for thy sake)
Will not grow bright and clean.

A servant with this clause
Makes drudgerie divine:
Who sweeps a room, as for thy laws,
Makes that and th'action fine.

This is the famous stone
That turneth all to gold:
For that which God doth touch and own
Cannot for lesse be told.

Lord, how can man preach thy eternall word?
    He is a brittle crazie glasse:
Yet in thy temple thou dost him afford
      This glorious and transcendent place,
      To be a window, through thy grace,

But when thou dost anneal in glasse thy storie,
    Making thy life to shine within
The holy Preachers; then the light and glorie
      More rev'rend grows, & more doth win:
      Which else shows watrish, bleak, & thin.

Doctrine and life, colours and light, in one
    When they combine and mingle, bring
A strong regard and awe: but speech alone
      Doth vanish like a flaring thing,
      And in the eare, not conscience ring.

Prayer is a source of strength in the life of obedience.

PRAYER I

Prayer the Churches banquet, Angels age,
>Gods breath in man returning to his birth,
>The soul in paraphrase, heart in pilgrimage,
The Christian plummet sounding heav'n and earth;

Engine against th' Almightie, sinners towre,
>Reversed thunder, Christ-side-piercing spear,
>The six-daies world-transposing in an houre,
A kinde of tune, which all things heare and fear;

Softnesse, and peace, and joy, and love, and blisse,
>Exalted Manna, gladnesse of the best,
>Heaven in ordinarie, man well drest,
The milkie way, the bird of Paradise,

>Church-bells beyond the starres heard, the souls
>bloud,
>The land of spices; something understood.

The Scriptures provide nourishment for the life of obedience.

THE HOLY SCRIPTURES I

Oh Book: infinite sweetnesse! let my heart
    Suck ev'ry letter, and a honey gain,
    Precious for any grief in any part;
To cleare the breast, to mollifie pain.

Thou art all health, health thriving till it make
    A full eternitie: thou art a masse
    Of strange delights, where we may wish and take.
Ladies, look here; this is the thankfull glasse,

That mends the lookers eyes: this is the well
    That washes what it shows. Who can indeare
    Thy praise too much? thou art heav'ns Lidger here,
Working against the states of death and hell.

    Thou art joyes handsell: heav'n lies flat in thee,
    Subject to ev'ry mounters bended knee.

The next two poems see daily worship as a means to obedience.

MATTENS

I cannot ope mine eyes,
But thou art ready there to catch
My morning-soul and sacrifice:
Then we must needs for that day make a match.

My God, what is a heart?
Silver, or gold, or precious stone,
Or starre, or rainbow, or a part
Of all these things, or all of them in one?

My God, what is a heart,
That thou shouldst it so eye, and wooe,
Powring upon it all thy art,
As if that thou hadst nothing els to do?

Indeed mans whole estate
Amounts (and richly) to serve thee:
He did not heav'n and earth create,
Yet studies them, not him by whom they be.

Teach me thy love to know;
That this new light, which now I see,
May both the work and workman show:
Then by a sunne-beam I will climbe to thee.

Blest be the God of love,
Who gave me eyes, and light, and power this day,
Both to be busie, and to play.
But much more blest be God above,

Who gave me sight alone,
Which to himself he did denie:
For when he sees my waies, I dy:
But I have got his sonne, and he hath none.

What have I brought thee home
For this thy love? have I discharg'd the debt,
Which this dayes favour did beget?
I ranne; but all I brought, was fome.

Thy diet, care, and cost
Do end in bubbles, balls of winde;
Of winde to thee whom I have crost,
But balls of wilde-fire to my troubled minde.

Yet still thou goest on.
And now with darknesse closest wearie eyes,
Saying to man, *It doth suffice*:
Henceforth repose; your work is done.

Thus in thy Ebony box
Thou dost inclose us, till the day
Put our amendment in our way,
And give new wheels to our disorder'd clocks.

I muse, which shows more love,
The day or night: that is the gale, this th' harbour;
That is the walk, and this the arbour;
Or that the garden, this the grove.

My God, thou art all love.
Not one poore minute scapes thy breast,
But brings a favour from above;
And in this love, more than in bed, I rest.

The great Christian Festivals as a means to obedience are the focus of the next two poems.

❀

CHRISTMAS

All after pleasures as I rid one day,
    My horse and I, both tir'd, bodie and minde,
    With full crie of affections, quite astray;
I took up in the next inne I could finde.

There when I came, whom found I but my deare,
    My dearest Lord, expecting till the grief
    Of pleasures brought me to him, readie there
To be all passengers most sweet relief?

O Thou, whose glorious, yet contracted light,
    Wrapt in nights mantle, stole into a manger;
    Since my dark soul and brutish is thy right,
To Man of all beasts be not thou a stranger:

    Furnish & deck my soul, that thou mayst have
    A better lodging, then a rack, or grave.

The shepherds sing; and shall I silent be?
    My God, no hymne for thee?
My soul's a shepherd too; a flock it feeds
    Of thoughts, and words, and deeds.
The pasture is thy word: the streams, thy grace
    Enriching all the place.
Shepherd and flock shall sing, and all my powers
    Out-sing the day-light houres.
Then we will chide the sunne for letting night
    Take up his place and right:
We sing one common Lord; wherefore he should
    Himself the candle hold.
I will go searching, till I finde a sunne
    Shall stay, till we have done;
A willing shiner, that shall shine as gladly,
    As frost-nipt sunnes look sadly.
Then we will sing, and shine all our own day,
    And one another pay:
His beams shall cheer my breast, and both so twine,
Till ev'n his beams sing, and my musick shine.

Rise heart; thy Lord is risen. Sing his praise
  Without delayes,
Who takes thee by the hand, that thou likewise
  With him mayst rise:
That, as his death calcined thee to dust,
His life may make thee gold, and much more just.

Awake, my lute, and struggle for thy part
  With all thy art.
The crosse taught all wood to resound his name,
  Who bore the same.
His streched sinews taught all strings, what key
Is best to celebrate this most high day.

Consort both heart and lute, and twist a song
  Pleasant and long:
Or since all musick is but three parts vied
  And multiplied;
O let thy blessed Spirit bear a part,
And make up our defects with his sweet art.

I got me flowers to straw thy way;
I got me boughs off many a tree:
But thou wast up by break of day,
And brought'st thy sweets along with thee.

The Sunne arising in the East,
Though he give light, & th' East perfume;
If they should offer to contest
With thy arising, they presume.

Can there be any day but this,
Though many sunnes to shine endeavour?
We count three hundred, but we misse:
There is but one, and that one ever.

EPILOGUE

The fruit of George Herbert's 'Lenten' life—a life of costly obedience—was a simple but absolute faith in, and love of, his Lord, such that it totally took over his thinking and doing and being. This final poem expresses the completeness and richness of the satisfaction he found in God.

THE CALL

Come, my Way, my Truth, my Life:
Such a Way, as gives us breath:
Such a Truth, as ends all strife:
And such a Life, as killeth death.

Come, my Light, my Feast, my Strength;
Such a Light, as shows a feast:
Such a Feast, as mends in length:
Such a Strength, as makes his guest.

Come, my Joy, my Love, my Heart:
Such a Joy, as none can move:
Such a Love, as none can part:
Such a Heart, as joyes in love.

NOTES

All poems in this book are taken from *The Temple, Sacred poems and private ejaculations,* published posthumously in 1633 with a text from Psalm 29 appended on the title page: 'In his Temple doth every man speak of his honour'. The poems within that collection are in three sections, 'The Church Porch', 'The Church', and 'The Church Militant'. All the poems in this selection are taken from the second section (though see note on 'Charms and Knots' below). The preface to *The Temple,* headed, 'The Printers to the Reader', was written by Nicolas Ferrars, a very close friend of Herbert and the leader of the Little Gidding community. (See Introduction.) Spelling has not been modernized, not least because some of Herbert's most delicate and subtle effects are in puns or rhymes dependent on the original spelling.

Introduction, page 8
From 'Deniall'
The cost to Herbert of God's silence is loss of his own music or poetry.

Introduction, page 8
'Charms and Knots'
Herbert's interest in proverbs reflects his pleasure both in neat and highly compressed profundities and in a certain worldly wisdom, which connects with his piety through his interest in wisdom literature. His collection of *Outlandish Proverbs* was published posthumously in 1640 (beginning, in Proverbs 1, with 'Man proposeth, God disposeth'). This was expanded in 1652, in his *Remains,* to *Jacula prudentum,* where the collection of 1032 proverbs was expanded by a further 158. In his poetry the lengthy poem 'Perirrhanterium', in the section 'The Church Porch' is built up on rhyming proverbs.

Page 12
'Antiphon I'
'Antiphon'—a passage sung alternately by two choirs, traditionally as part of worship.

Page 13
'Antiphon II'
The original title of 'Antiphon II' was 'Ode'.

Page 17
'Affliction I'
Line 53: 'crosse-bias me': 'make me change direction': a picture drawn from the game of bowls.

Page 20
'The Collar'
Line 17 '...there is fruit/And thou hast hands': a reference to Adam and Eve choosing to be disobedient by taking the fruit. The poet declares he has the option of doing the same: why should he remain in painful obedience?

Page 21
'Sinnes round'
Based on a 'round', a song with repeated lines which could go on for ever—as could his sin...

Page 23
'Affliction IV'
Original title: 'Tentation' (i.e. 'Temptation').

Page 28
'Love III'
This—perhaps his best-loved poem—concludes the second and major section of Herbert's poetry, 'The Church'; a 'parable' poem.

Page 31
'Praise II'
Based on Psalm 116; Herbert uses the first line as the basis of the last poem ('Love's Envoy') in his complete poems.

Page 32
'JESU'
Based on an anagram; Herbert is using a form of wit popularized in Tudor poetry, equally popular in the twentieth century.

Page 33
'Redemption'
Original title 'The Passion'. One of a number of verse 'parables' (see 'Love III' above).

Page 34
'Good Friday'
Original title to lines 21-32 (as in 'Redemption' above), 'The Passion'.

Page 35
'The Dawning'
The title is a pun: the 'dawning' is both of Easter understanding on the part of Christ's followers, and of Easter Day itself. (See 'Easter Wings' and 'Easter'.)

Page 36
'Easter Wings'
One of several examples of 'pattern poetry' in Herbert's verse. (See 'Paradise'.)

Page 39
'The Windows'
Another sharply imaginative image, where clergy are presented as stained-glass windows, whose full glory is only seen when what they *say*, their 'doctrine', is shone through by the glory of God himself within them, i.e. what they *do*—their 'life'.

Page 41
'The Holy Scriptures I'
See 'The Printers to the Reader'—preface to Herbert's poems by his friend Nicolas Ferrars, who comments, 'Next God, he loved that which God Himself hath magnified above all things, that is, His Word.'